CW01512923

# Practical NLP

*How to use NLP principles to improve your life and work, even if you're not NLP trained*

Book 1 in the *Practical NLP* series

ANDY SMITH

Copyright © 2017 Andy Smith
All rights reserved.
ISBN: 1979979189
ISBN-13: 978-1979979184

# CONTENTS

# INTRODUCTION

*"First, you know, a new theory is attacked as absurd; then it is admitted to be true, but obvious and insignificant; finally it is seen to be so important that its adversaries claim that they themselves discovered it."*

## - William James, *Pragmatism: A New Name for Some Old Ways of Thinking* (1907)

### What this book is *not* about

This book is not about how to learn NLP, since it's generally agreed that to get anywhere near mastering the skills of NLP so you can use them successfully to help yourself or other people, you need to attend a reasonably lengthy live training course that allows for lots of practice and gives you continual feedback from someone who knows what they are doing.

### What this book *is* about

Rather, this book is about how you can apply the principles or 'presuppositions' of NLP ('presuppositions' just means the basic ideas that you have to assume or 'presuppose' to be true in order to be able to use NLP and make it work for you). This is something that you *can* learn from a book, as long as you take the time to actually try out the practical exercises in each section.

Calling these ideas 'principles of NLP' might be taken to imply that they are actually true, or that they are some kind of belief system that you are expected to take on trust, but that's not the intention.

In NLP we're not concerned about making generalisations about what is true or not; rather, we're concerned with what works and what is useful. We're not asking you to believe these presuppositions as articles of faith; we're asking you to act *as if* they are true in order to make NLP work for you, and very soon you'll start generating your own evidence that they work.

## Why a book about principles?

Here's the big question: why write (or read) a book on just the principles of NLP, that doesn't go into the details of specific techniques, models, and specialist terms that you see in so many NLP books?

On the many NLP courses that I've attended, assisted on, or run as a trainer, I've noticed time and again that many of the biggest breakthroughs for the participants ('light bulb moments', 'aha moments', call them what you will) happen early on in the course, before people have really learned any 'NLP techniques', just from understanding the NLP presuppositions and how life looks different in the light of them.

I've had participants on my NLP Practitioner courses tell me that applying maybe just one of these presuppositions has made a massive positive difference in their lives. Maybe you will have the same experience.

## So are these principles true or not?

In their early seminars Richard Bandler and John Grinder, the originators of NLP, used to say 'Everything we're about to tell you is a lie' - which usually got people's attention. The thing is, anything that any trainer tells you will be a lie to the extent that they are making generalisations, because you can always find an exception somewhere. The real question is not 'Are these statements true?' but 'Are they useful?'

## Why isn't there one definitive list of NLP presuppositions?

In every book you read about NLP, you'll find a slightly different list of these presuppositions - they're all saying the same thing in different ways. The reason you get differing formulations is perhaps because as far as I know, Bandler and Grinder didn't set down all of them, so there hasn't been a definitive set handed down by the originators of NLP. Some versions of the presuppositions were set down by people they trained and worked with, such as Robert Dilts. And, of course, every NLP trainer wants to get the presuppositions across in the way that will work for their students, so you find many slightly different versions - all expressing the same basic ideas.

## About the term 'presupposition' in NLP

I should point out that the word 'presupposition' also has a broader meaning in NLP, covering anything that's presupposed in a question or statement. For example, in the classic sales closing question "Would you like to pay by cash or card?" presupposes that you are going to buy, even though it doesn't explicitly say that. If you go for either of the two choices on offer, 'cash' or 'card', you've already accepted the presupposition.

With NLP we can become more aware of this kind of presupposition in our own language so we can become better communicators. We can also become more aware of them in other people's language, so they can't manipulate us so easily.

## Why these principles are useful

Returning to presuppositions in the 'principles of NLP' sense, the useful thing about them is that you can use them to make your life better without any formal training or skills in NLP.

Obviously you will get even better results if you do get some training and develop some skills, but acting 'as if' the principles are true will still help you. This is because the principles are an attitude and a way of looking at the world that you can regard as a set of instructions for success.

The version of the NLP presuppositions that I've found works best is something I've adapted from a slightly longer set by Richard Bolstad, a great NLP trainer from New Zealand. To make them easier to remember, Richard grouped them into presuppositions about people, and presuppositions about communication and making changes or assisting others with change. In our adaptation there are six presuppositions in each category. Let's start with presuppositions about people.

# PRINCIPLES ABOUT PEOPLE

*"Trust yourself, then you will know how to live."*
**- Johann Wolfgang von Goethe (1749 - 1832)**

*"The universe is change; our life is what our thoughts make it."*
**- Marcus Aurelius Antoninus (121 - 180),** *Meditations*

*"The mind is its own place, and in it self*
*Can make a Heav'n of Hell, a Hell of Heav'n."*
**- John Milton (1608 - 1674),** *Paradise Lost*

*"If you could kick the person in the pants responsible for most of your*
*trouble, you wouldn't sit for a month."*
-    **Theodore Roosevelt, US President 1901-1909**

Understanding and applying these principles about how we as human beings operate will make a big and worthwhile difference to your own personal development.

# 1

## "The map is not the territory"

This is the single most important presupposition of NLP, and the one that many of the other presuppositions spring from. What it comes down to is this: people respond and make choices based not on absolute reality, but according to how they perceive the world.

### Mental filters

Our conscious awareness has a limited number of 'chunks of attention' (around 7, many people say, citing the psychologist George Miller's famous paper *The Magical Number 7±2*, but in practice it's probably more like 3 or 4).

So in order to make sense of the huge amount of information that our senses take in each moment from the world around us, we unconsciously filter it.

We have to do this filtering. If we didn't, our brains would be overloaded and the world would appear as a blooming, buzzing riot of smells, feelings and colours, just as it must appear to a new-born baby.

Here are some of the filtering processes that our brain uses to protect us:

### Deletion

We just don't notice certain things, especially if we are not interested in them. So in every situation, there is more going on than you realise. Most of the information we delete may be irrelevant, but sometimes we overlook things that would help us if we noticed them.

In fact, one of the ways that psychedelic drugs like mescaline or LSD work is that, in Aldous Huxley's phrase, they open *"The Doors of Perception"* - in other words, they take away the filters that are normally in place. So if you have that familiar image from the sixties of a hippy who's taken LSD, sitting for hours staring at a leaf, going 'Oh wow....' it's not so much that the acid is making him hallucinate things on the leaf, it's more that the information from the leaf that we normally filter out is allowed through, and there's more than enough sensory information from just one leaf to occupy the brain for hours.

So in normal life, our brains have to perform this Deletion. If they didn't, we would just be overwhelmed by information, and we would never get round to doing anything. If we didn't filter incoming information, we wouldn't be able to process it fast enough to do simple things like crossing a road - we'd still be standing there hours later, as small animals come up and start nibbling us. So Deletion is an essential process to survival - but sometimes, we delete things that it would actually be useful to notice, and that can cause problems.

## Distortion
Psychologists have identified various 'cognitive biases' that distort our view of the world:

"Confirmation Bias" - we pay more attention to evidence that supports our beliefs, and downplay or ignore evidence that doesn't.

The "Bandwagon Effect" - we are more likely to do or believe something when we see many other people doing or believing it.

The "Illusion of Control" - we believe we can control or influence outcomes, even when we can't.

The "Halo Effect" - if we like one quality or trait of a person or thing, we tend to view their other qualities or traits more favourably.

## Generalisation
We look for commonality and predictability. What we expect to happen is influenced by our perceptions of previous events. For example, gamblers and stock market investors tend to see a 'winning streak' after three good results, even though 'streaks' are a natural feature of any random sequence (see "The Rule of Three" on the British Psychological Society's Research Digest blog).

## What's important about a map
Usually, these 'cognitive shortcuts' work in our favour. Thinking is time-consuming, and expensive in energy terms. If we had to think every single thing we did through from first principles, we would be unable to act at all.

But sometimes, these shortcuts work against us - we miss relevant information, jump to conclusions, or view people through a lens of prejudice.

The result of our knowledge being 'filtered' is that we end up with an internal representation of the world around us that bears the same relationship to reality as a map does to the territory that it depicts. I can't emphasise strongly enough - *this internal representation is all we know.* By the time we become aware of information coming in from the world around us, the information has already been through our filters.

So the world we perceive is not reality - it's our filtered representation of reality. Now you might say that therefore everything is an illusion, and reality is hidden from us, since what we see is not the absolute truth.

Here's the thing: with a map, it doesn't matter if it's true - it matters if it's useful. Think about all the different kinds of map there are: road maps, street A-Zs, relief maps, maps showing population density, weather patterns, languages spoken, geology, which religions are practiced in which areas, animal migrations, temperature bands... Are any of these maps absolutely true? No - but some of them are more useful than others, depending on how closely they correspond to the territory they depict, and on what you want to accomplish with them ...as people have found out in the past.

## The Kingdom Of The Mapmakers

*There was once a kingdom renowned for the excellence of its mapmakers. Such was the accuracy, detail and beauty of their maps that each time you looked at one you would discover something new.*

*One day the Guild of Cartographers came to the king and presented their proposal for the ultimate map of the kingdom - a map that would show not only rivers and towns, political boundaries and forests, but heights above sea level, languages spoken, geological composition of the earth, animal and plant species, prevailing winds, predominant religions, rainfall levels, trades and industries, average temperatures, the migrations of birds...*

*The king, appreciative of their skill and knowledge, and mindful of how the map would secure the prestige of the kingdom, gave them a huge chest of gold to fund the project.*

*Some centuries later (for the project took longer than expected, as the inevitable changes in the kingdom had to be redrawn into the map), the descendants of the*

*Cartographers' Guild came to the then king, a distant descendant of the first one, with their finished map.*

*"Right," said the king, "unroll it on the banqueting table and let's have a look."*

*"Sorry sire," said the mapmakers, "in order to accommodate all the detail we've had to make it a very large-scale map, and it's too big to unroll on the table."*

*"Fine," said the king, "you courtiers move the table out of the way and we'll unroll it on the throne room floor."*

*"I am afraid, sire," said the head of the Cartographer's Guild, "to show all of the parish boundaries, family ties, varieties of fruit grown, and mineral deposits - not to mention the one-way streets and the historic monuments - we've had to make it on too large a scale for the throne room to accommodate it."*

*"Right," said the king, beginning to get a little tetchy, "we'll clear the soldiers from the parade ground outside and they can unroll it."*

*"Sire, we had to make it on a very big scale to accurately capture all the detail - I'm afraid there will not be sufficient room on the parade ground."*

*"Well what scale is it man?" roared the king. "One in a thousand, one in five hundred, what?"*

*"Errm... In order to accommodate all the detail, we had to make it... one to one scale, sire."*

*... and to this day, if you visit the desert where the kingdom used to be, you can still see tattered scraps of the ultimate map blowing in the desolate breeze.*

If that story seems vaguely familiar, I'll confess right now that it's inspired by Jorge Luis Borges' story *On Exactitude in Science*. If you haven't read any Borges up till now, I strongly recommend that you do - his stories are thought-provoking and they're really short, usually just a few pages. That one is just one paragraph long.

## Implications of the map not being the territory

What you experience is not reality. By the time you become aware of experiencing something, it's already been filtered. So your 'reality', as you are experiencing it right now, is subject to the deletions, distortions and generalisations of your filters.

A good map is one that is useful. Since all maps leave out information, the real issue is not "Is this map true?" but "Is this map useful?" A map is useful to the extent that it helps you accomplish what you want to do; if you're assessing where floods might occur, a rainfall map may be what you want, but if you want to get to a particular place, you're going to need a road map. In either case you're going to want a map that corresponds to the territory and doesn't lead you astray.

Yours is not the only truth. Each person has a different viewpoint. They will notice things that you have missed, and vice versa. Their view of 'reality' is as valid to them as yours is to you. People who believe that everyone sees the world in the same way that they do are setting themselves up for constant bewilderment; people who believe that others should see the world as they do are setting themselves up for constant disappointment.

People's actions make sense from their map, which we can never fully know or understand. Often their actions would seem crazy or wrong when judged in the context of our map - so when coaching or communicating with them, suspend judgment.

Since we all have different maps, no one map is more "real" or "true" than another - although some maps may be more useful in terms of helping you to find your way round the world.

People get into difficulties if they lose that map/territory distinction and start to confuse their perception with reality. It's as if they've gone into a restaurant, looked at the menu and thought, "That looks tasty" - and then started to eat the menu! So - another NLP saying - don't eat the menu.

Linked to that map/territory confusion is another trap that people sometimes fall into: assuming that everyone else has the same map as them. People make choices that make sense according to their own maps of the world. If you are operating from a different map, sometimes those choices won't make sense to you, and vice versa. If someone thinks that everyone shares their map, they are bound to be puzzled by or disappointed in other people quite a lot of the time.

And even if people intellectually recognise that their map is not the absolute truth, and that other people have different maps, they can still create a lot of trouble for themselves if they believe that other people 'should' have the same map.

# Practical ways to make this principle work for you

## 1. See other people's point of view

When you have a disagreement with someone, or you just don't understand why they have done something, put yourself in their shoes and look at the world, and yourself, from their point of view. Aim to adopt their map rather than just thinking 'What would I do in that situation?' You will get better-quality information if you match their 'physiology' (the term often used in NLP for general stance and body language) - so to match someone's physiology, stand as they stand, breathe as they breathe, move at the same speed that they do, and so on.

To avoid the cognitive error of 'mind-reading', which is where people talk and act as if they know for sure what someone else is thinking or feeling, remember that the intuitions you get from this exercise are just a guess about what the other person is thinking and feeling. Always check out your intuitions against what the person actually does.

## 2. To influence someone, start from their map of the world

When you want to persuade someone to change their mind, don't expect them to jump straight to your map. Why would anyone want to do that? Instead, start from a position that makes sense to them and is compatible with their values and beliefs, and build bridges to the place you want the person to get to.

Think of someone you have been trying to influence or change their mind, without much success so far. Which of their values or beliefs could have been getting in the way of the change you want them to make? And which of their values or beliefs might help move them towards where you want them to be?

## 3. Explore the boundaries of your map

Where are the limits of your map? What do you feel you can't do, or that you don't deserve? The areas in your life that are not going as well as you would like may indicate that your map could do with some tweaks. So:

   a) where you have a belief that is holding you back or not serving you - like some people stop themselves from exercising because they believe they are no good at sport - actively look for examples where that belief is not true.

b) where you tend to make generalisations, actively look for counter-examples. There are always going to be exceptions to any generalisation... including this one.

c) when you think you can't do something that you would like to do, ask yourself "What would happen if I did?"

Which leads us logically to the next presupposition:

# 2

## All behaviour is the best choice currently available

If people have their own internal representations or maps of the world, and they make choices according to those maps and not to reality, it follows that the choices they make are going to be the ones that make the most sense in their map. These are the best choices available to them. There may have been other choices they could make, but if those choices weren't in their map, they won't even see them.

Notice that this presupposition doesn't say that the choices you make are objectively the best choice, or the one you would have picked if you had the benefit of hindsight.

This idea has a couple of interesting implications. Firstly, if you did something in the past that you now regrct, that means you have learned something from it - if you would now act differently in the same situation. You were doing the best you could with the resources available to you at that time; now, with your enriched and expanded map, you would act differently. So there's no point beating yourself up about your past decision; the important thing is to learn from your mistakes so you do better next time.

Of course, you are still responsible for your actions. So you still have a responsibility to continue to enrich and improve your map, so that you increase your ability to make better choices.

If you've ever given up smoking multiple times, or continued to overeat at the same time as wanting to be slimmer and fitter, or put off preparing for an important presentation or work project even though you actually want to get it done, you may have wondered "If all behaviour is the best choice currently available, why do I still do things that aren't good for me?"

These kinds of problem behaviours might be unwanted habits like smoking or overeating, or inappropriate emotional responses like excessive outbursts of anger, or persistent unfounded anxiety. How can that problem behaviour be the best choice available?

The answer is that the problem behaviour or habit is the best choice the person has been able to find so far; there's some kind of benefit or payoff to the behaviour that they wouldn't get if they stopped. This applies just as much to organisational change as it does to individual change.

Sometimes it's as if a part of the mind that sees the world differently from conscious awareness, with different filters and different values, is responsible for a problem behaviour, and keeps the person doing the behaviour, and even though consciously they would like to stop, they don't. Anyone who has given up smoking multiple times will know what I mean.

Secondly, if behaviour is the best choice currently available, that means that other people are doing the best they are able to as well. It's harder to hate or despise other people, and easier to feel compassion for them, when you remember that just like you, they are doing the best that they can given the way that they see the world.

Another way you often see this NLP presupposition stated is "There is a positive intention behind every behaviour" - 'positive' in the sense that it's trying to achieve something or get some benefit for that person, not necessarily for anyone else. When you want to change behaviour like this you need to separate the intention - which is positive - from the behaviour, which may well have 'negative' or damaging results.

## Practical ways to make this principle work for you

### 1. What have you learned?

If there's something you did in the past that you regret - what would you do differently if that happened next time? What positive lessons have you learned from it?

If there is any emotional pain, or guilt, still attached to the memory, that means there is still something to be learned. So, when the time is right, ask yourself "Now what do I need to learn from that event in order to let go of that emotion and move beyond it?" Shine the light of your attention on to what you would do differently now. Take your mental image of the positive lessons you've learned and the ways in which you would behave differently and make it big, bright and clear. Now any time you remember that event, you can also see the valuable lessons you've learned and how you will act differently.

## 2. What is the positive intention of the problem?

If you've been doing some habit that you want to change, like smoking or overeating, or if you have something like a critical inner voice, or if you have any sort of problem that hasn't been easy to solve - and you may find this even works for health problems in some cases - suppose for a moment that there's a positive intention behind it.

Of course, the results may not be positive for you, but just for a moment suppose that there is a positive intention behind the problem, or that there's a payoff or benefit in some sense that the problem or habit is trying to give you.

So what is that problem or habit trying to do for you, as well as it currently knows how? Take a moment to think about it. How else could you get that benefit, once you let go of that habit or problem? Maybe you can think of three or four possible ways to get a similar benefit - or better - without the negative effects of the problem or habit.

## 3. Apply the principle to other people as well

This will be a big one for some readers, but "all behaviour is the best choice currently available" applies to other people as well. So when other people do things you don't like, even the worst things, they are doing it because it seems to them, with their map of the world, like the best choice available.

Getting angry about what other people do, if the anger doesn't spur you to take action to resolve the conflict or get them to change what they're doing, only affects you. Especially if the reason you're getting angry is because they 'should' be doing something else, according to your map and your values.

So if there's someone out there who you really dislike - it could be a neighbour, or a public figure, or a close family member - try this exercise:

    a) Think of that person - see them in your mind's eye. Notice how you feel, without getting sucked into the feeling.

Observe the feeling from a distance, knowing that it will pass like every other thought and feeling.

b) Briefly put yourself in that person's shoes, having had their upbringing, seeing the world as they see it.

Now come back to yourself and look at that person again, and say to yourself: "Just like me, they are doing the best they can." Notice any changes in how you feel. And bring everything that you've learned back with you as you come back to normal awareness.

# 3

## People have all the resources they need to succeed

If you are managing someone, or teaching them, or coaching them, this presupposition matters, because your expectations of who they are and what they are capable of will actually influence their performance.

### "Pygmalion in the Classroom"

Studies have been supporting this idea for decades. In the 1960s, Harvard psychology professor Robert Rosenthal set up an experiment where elementary school teachers were told that certain children were likely to show signs of a spurt in intellectual development. Sure enough, at the end of the year, the children in the experimental group showed a significant gain in IQ points over the control group - but in fact, the children had been selected at random! The only difference was the teachers' expectations.

What's more, when children in the so-called 'lower track' started to show unexpected signs of intellectual improvement, their teacher evaluations marked them down on things like 'personal adjustment', 'happiness' and 'affectionate'.

Similar results have been reproduced in higher education, in management, and even with researchers' expectations of laboratory animals. The lesson is that if you are teaching, or managing, or coaching someone, your expectations of their potential will become self-fulfilling prophesies, especially if they look up to you and respect you. This is also true of your expectations of yourself. Expect the best, and you will be more likely to get it.

### Resourceful and unresourceful states

Another way of putting this presupposition is that there are no unresourceful people, only unresourceful states. We all have amazing and tremendously capable brains, capable of logic, planning and rational decisions. Your brain contains around a billion neurons, or brain cells, and I'm reliably informed that the total number of potential pathways through the brain is in the region of 3 x 10^5,000,000,000 - or more than the total number of atoms in the known universe.

The cerebral cortex, which is the wrinkly surface that you see in any diagram of the brain, is the part of the brain that does that rational thinking; in each one of us, it has the ability to look at things from different perspectives, make new connections, reframe events, and put things into perspective. That's how we normally get over shocks and upsets, and also how we get new ideas.

Just because we have these amazing brains, it doesn't mean we always use them. Remember when Mike Tyson bit off part of Evander Holyfield's ear in the WBA Heavyweight Boxing championship in 1997? Or when Zinedine Zidane head-butted Marco Materazzi in the 2006 World Cup final, quite probably leading to his team losing? Or any incident of road rage?

As well as the cerebral cortex, we also have older parts of the brain that process fight or flight responses and emotions - sometimes known as the lizard brain and the horse brain respectively, because the structures are pretty similar in us and other animals. When we are in the grip of a strong emotion like rage or panic, the thinking part of the brain pretty much shuts down, and people think and act like a cornered animal. They forget about nuances and adopting different viewpoints and see things in an all-or-nothing, black and white way. "Strong emotions make us stupid" as neuroscientist Joseph LeDoux points out.

So it doesn't matter how intelligent or capable someone is - if they are in an unresourceful state, they won't be able to get the results they want. NLP gives you practical ways of accessing resourceful states, and so being able to get the results you want.

### That's easy for you to say...

Now some readers may be thinking, "'Everyone has all the resources they need to succeed' - that's easy for a university-educated middle-aged white guy to say. Some people really don't have a chance because of social conditions." The thing is, no matter what restrictions of class, wealth, gender or disability you care to name, you will find someone who has transcended them - whether it's Nelson Mandela coming back from 18 years hard labour on Robben

Island, and a total of 27 years in prison, to become president of South Africa and guide the country peacefully through the transition from white minority rule; or JK Rowling moving from single mother on benefits to multi-millionaire best-selling author within five years; or Helen Keller, left deaf and blind by an illness she contracted at 19 months, who went on to become the author of 12 published books, the first deafblind person to earn a Bachelor of Arts degree, and one of the most admired people of the 20th Century.

People are not limited to the resources just within themselves. How would you like to work in a dangerous environment, 12 hours a day, six days a week, with no paid leave, and be paid just enough - if you're lucky - to survive? That was the common experience of industrial workers in the western world in the 19th Century, and is still the case for many of the people in poorer countries who make your clothes and consumer goods today

Individually, those people had very few resources. Collectively, when they organised into unions, they were strong, and gradually, with a lot of determination and hard work, they wrung concessions from their employers that led to the more humane and productive working conditions we enjoy today.

Because of where it started (America) and the personalities of the original developers, NLP has always had a strong emphasis on individual responsibility. *And* there are a lot of collective resources available out there as well. Together, we can achieve more than we can working individually, and, in the words of Douglas Merrill, former Chief Information Officer of Google, all of us are smarter than any of us. So - if and when you need it - where can you find additional resources, of information, ideas, help, and emotional support, from your friends, family, workmates, and the wider society around you?

Just as in the 'Pygmalion in the Classroom' experiment, when people think of themselves or others as limited, they run the risk of putting artificial ceilings on what they can achieve. Start from the presupposition that people have all the resources they need to succeed, and you make success much more likely.

# Practical ways to make this principle work for you

## 1. Discover what's already working and build on it

Since your emotional state influences how much of your resources you can access, it makes sense to remember and inquire into the times when things went well if you're wanting to improve your performance. This is one aspect of a method called Appreciative Inquiry, which shares a lot of assumptions with NLP.

If there's something you want to improve about your performance in a particular area, and nothing else has worked, try this - either get a friend to ask you these questions, or if you're on your own, write your answers:

Tell me about your best time in this area, a time that you performed better than usual, you felt alive and engaged, and you learned something positive about yourself.

What's important to you about this story?

What was it about that situation, about the people around or about you, that made this better performance possible?

If you had one wish for the future about this area, what would it be?

## 2. Transfer resources from other contexts

What skills or qualities have you shown in other areas of your life that could help you in the areas you want to improve?

## 3. Who are you when you are at your best?

Ask yourself this question, or get a friend who is a good listener to ask you, and see what comes up. You may surprise yourself, and you will probably discover a deeper connection to your true self and purpose.

## 4. Ask other people to find the strengths you've missed

Since we tend to take our own strengths for granted: what do other people say your strengths are, even if you think it's no big deal yourself?

## 5. You're not alone

Who else, and where else, can you get help from?

## 6. Get into the right state first

Again, since you have access to more of your resources when you're in a positive emotional state, what could you do to get yourself into the right state before you tackle something important? (hint: taking a moment to pause and centre yourself is usually a good idea)

## 7. Remember the Pygmalion Effect

If you're managing, coaching, or teaching someone else, remember that they have all the resources they need. If you've put a label on them of 'stupid', or 'lazy', or 'negative', remember that this acts as a filter on your perception of their performance, so it tends to become a self-fulfilling prophecy. So remember that they have all the resources they need, and actively look for evidence that challenges your existing judgement of them. You may be pleasantly surprised by an improvement in their performance.

# 4

## I am in charge of my mind, and therefore my results

This is essentially about taking responsibility for your own actions, and finding ways to be the best you can. If you have all the resources that you need, if mind and body are one system, and if your state is a response to your internal representation of the world, then you can put yourself in the best state to get results by what you do and the way that you think.

### Cause and Effect

As human beings, we tend to see the world in terms of causes and effects. If something we do consistently gets a certain result, we say that our action causes that result. If one event is consistently followed by another, we start believing that the first event causes the second.

This is a useful way of looking at things when applied to simple relationships between inanimate objects: you kick a football, and that causes it to fly into the back of the net. An engineer who knows the mass of the football, the speed and angle at which you kick it, and the wind speed, could pretty much predict exactly where the ball is going to end up. This idea is known as 'determinism': if you know the initial conditions, you can predict exactly what's going to happen next. It all happens predictably, like clockwork.

That deterministic worldview is not so useful when applied to living things: if you kick a gorilla, what's the gorilla going to do? The answer is - whatever it wants to. It could ignore you and stay still, it could obligingly scoot along the ground and into the goalmouth; or, it could pick you up and throw you into the back of the net. There's a lot going on in the gorilla's internal processing between the initial event (your kick) and the end result.

Determinism is even less useful when applied to human beings. If everything was determined by what has happened previously, then free will would be an illusion, and our destinies would be predetermined by our situations, our upbringing, and our genes. We would definitely be placing ourselves at the 'effect' end of the equation.

In contrast, when you move to the 'cause' side of the equation, you believe "I can make a difference; I can make things happen; I am responsible for how I feel and for where I am". In answer to NLP co-founder Richard Bandler's question of "Who's driving the bus?", you can say, "I am!".

Putting yourself 'at cause' is about taking responsibility - recognising that *you have the ability*, the 'response ability', to *respond*, rather than just react, to whatever life throws at you. *You can make things happen; you have the power to change things*; the 'locus of control', as psychologists call it, is within you rather than outside of you.

If you think the 'cause' end of the equation sounds like a better, more exciting, more empowering place to be than the 'effect' end, I agree with you. You may have noticed how many people do seem to place themselves at 'effect'. The idea that other people are responsible for how we feel and act is even built into the English language: "He made me angry" or "She upset me". Even inanimate objects can apparently do it - take for example a car not starting: "This faulty starter motor is really winding me up!"

When people think like this, they are accepting a belief that emotions are things which just happen to us, or that other people cause in us. So they act as if they have no responsibility for what they feel. Sometimes they even believe that other people are even responsible for what they do. I had a client once who wanted help with managing his anger. If another man looked at him in a certain way, he believed that he had no choice but to hit him - a belief that had eventually landed him in court.

So, people who place themselves at the 'effect' end of the equation - and from what I see this is most people, most of the time - are in effect saying "I am not responsible for what I feel or how I react; everyone else is." They have given their power away. Somehow, those other people - or even inanimate objects, in the case of cash machines that won't pay out or cars that won't start - have caused the release of certain chemicals called neuropeptides within that person's body which fit into the appropriate receptors in the surface of their brain cells and "cause" them to feel a certain way.

That's quite a degree of control, especially if it's a lump of metal doing it.

Things get even stranger at the 'effect' end of the equation: when people are there, they believe that they not responsible for your own emotions, but they are, apparently, responsible for everyone else's. That means they get to feel guilty whenever someone else says, "You've really upset me!" Since most people don't like feeling guilty and will go to some lengths to avoid it, that means the other person has a way of manipulating them, just by saying "You've made me feel bad".

We've all been there. A stimulus or trigger (whatever the other person, or object, did) is followed, apparently instantly, by the emotional response. This happens so quickly that it feels like one causes the other.

Now actually, as the late Stephen Covey points out in his book *The 7 Habits of Highly Effective People*, there's a lot going on between the stimulus and the response. The stimulus could be what that other person does, or something they say, or the tone of voice in which they say it, or the look on their face.

In order for it to register as a stimulus at all, your mind has to interpret it as something threatening, provoking or guilt inducing, probably by matching it to the memories of previous bad experiences that it might remind you of. You have to evaluate the incoming sensory information in the light of your existing belief system. Maybe you have to tell yourself something about the stimulus that labels it as cheeky, insolent, aggressive, or inappropriate, before you get to feel the bad emotional response.

All this happens at an unconscious level, in a fraction of a second - and the more times you do it, the quicker it happens. Like anything else, you get better with practice - your brain forms new neural pathways which are widened and strengthened with every repetition, so the message to set off the response can whip along them faster and faster. You're not consciously aware of this process. As a result, it really does feel like the stimulus is causing the next thing you're aware of - the unresourceful emotional response.

The psychologist Viktor Frankl was imprisoned in Auschwitz and other concentration camps for five years. In that situation he saw the worst of humanity in the behaviour of the guards. Many of his fellow prisoners gave up, or acted as if they had abandoned all human feeling in the struggle to survive, as we would expect in such a terrible predicament. But Frankl observed other prisoners who, despite being in the worst place in the world, were still able to find meaning in their lives and could still act with kindness and courage. What he saw of the best and worst in people in the camps inspired him to move away from Freud's belief that the driving forces of our actions are instincts and urges; instead, he came to believe that man's deepest desire is to search for meaning and purpose. Later he wrote the great book *Man's Search for Meaning*, in which he says, "Between stimulus and response there is a space. In that space is our power to choose our response. In our response lies our growth and our freedom."

Following on from that idea, Stephen Covey says, "Quality of life depends on what happens in the space between stimulus and response". What NLP will give you is some practical ways to choose what happens between stimulus and response - and the more you exercise and develop that choice, the more your freedom to choose increases, and the more you move over to the 'cause' side of the equation.

The other thing that's worth noticing about cause and effect is this: when someone is at the effect end of the equation, it makes them less effective at dealing with the curveballs that life occasionally throws at us. If someone says or does something unpleasant to a person at 'effect', the questions that person asks to make sense of what's happened are probably going to start with "Why?" "Why are they being so horrible to me? Why does this always happen to me?" The question "why" focuses their attention towards the past; if you believe that where you are now is caused entirely by external forces, your upbringing, and your genes, then of course they are going to look for past causes in order to understand the problem.

In contrast, when you place yourself at cause, and something happens that you don't like, what kind of questions are you likely to be asking yourself as you start to make sense of what's happened? They are more likely to be questions such as: "What's going on here? How has this come about? What can I do to change things?" or even "What do I want instead of this in the future?"

Rather than focusing on the past, that by its nature is over with and done, the questions you ask when you are 'at cause' focus your attention on what's happening now, where you can actually do something to make a difference, and on what you want to change in the future. They focus on solutions rather than the details of problems, and with any challenge except the very simplest ones, they are more helpful to get to where you want to be.

Of course, I'm not suggesting that putting yourself at cause will make your life perfect; you're still going to encounter challenges along the way. But the more you place yourself at cause, the more resourceful and effective you will be in meeting them, and the more you will learn from overcoming any challenge. It's a much more empowering place to be.

## Choices

In principle you can overcome any limitation; of course, this doesn't mean that it will always be easy, or that you won't decide that the energy it takes to overcome a limitation would be better used elsewhere. You always have a choice.

You are also in charge of improving your mind, so you can get better results in the future. You have a choice about what you learn about and how you spend your time. Just as an example, someone who has watched every episode of 'Eastenders' has given over 2,300 hours of their life so far to learning about the notoriously depressing lives of fictional characters in a soap opera. Is that the best use of their time? They, like you, had a choice.

In the end, it comes down to Richard Bandler's question - "Who's driving the bus?"

# Practical ways to make this principle work for you

### 1. If something happens that you don't like...

Ask yourself "What's going on here? Where can I make a difference? What do I want instead of this in the future?"

### 2. Identify what you would like more of in your life, and what you would like less of

If nothing changed in your situation, what changes could you make in your actions and what you pay attention to that would start improving things? What are you giving your time, attention or energy to which could be better spent elsewhere? Examples might be - money spent on a daily paper or cappuccino, time spent on social networks or watching TV, attention given to problems and complaints while your achievements and the things you love are ignored.

### 3. If you're blaming someone else for problems in your life...
Ask yourself: "What is the most useful thing I can do about this now?" and "What would happen if I take responsibility?"

### 4. In any situation at all...
Ask yourself: "What's the right thing to do?"

### 5. If you're ever anxious, stressed or unhappy...
Ask yourself: "What am I most resisting doing right now?"

### 6. When facing a challenge...
Ask yourself: "What do I need to do to put myself in the best state to handle this?"

### 7. If you're feeling uninspired or you're putting off doing something...
Ask yourself: "What's the smallest thing I can do right now to move towards where I want to be?"

Many of these make great coaching questions as well.

# 5

## The only reliable information about a person is their behaviour

Have you ever tried to compliment someone and they've taken it the wrong way? Or had someone tell you "Now just calm down" when you weren't actually annoyed (or not until they told you to calm down anyway)?

What's happening there is that the person has taken something that they've noticed about what you're doing, interpreted it through their own mental filters, and come to the wrong conclusion about your intentions, or about what you are thinking and feeling. In NLP, this is known as 'mind-reading' - they can't actually read your mind, but they are acting as if they can.

Pretty much everyone does that from time to time. In fact, our unconscious minds are mostly pretty good at reading non-verbal signals and using that information to guess at someone's state, so you can get an idea of what they might do next, when to back off, when is a good time to ask them for something, and so on.

However, our perceptions are not infallible. Sometimes, because our filters delete, distort and generalise incoming information, or because we might project unrecognised emotions of our own onto the other person, we get it wrong.

Going back to the person who tells you to calm down when you're not annoyed: if you tell them that actually you are calm, and they refuse to believe it, trusting their own intuition over the evidence, and continue to insist that you are angry, what would you think of them? The chances are that you wouldn't place much trust in their judgement, since they don't seem to have a feedback loop to update their first impression with new information.

They might go on to tell you that they are a very intuitive person and they are never wrong about how a person is feeling. Would you believe them, and start thinking 'Oh actually, I must be angry, even though I'm not aware of feeling anger"?

It seems unlikely. But you might want to check your body language, just in case. If you find that your fists are clenched, and your teeth are gritted, and you look in the mirror and find you are frowning intensely, you might modify your opinion on whether you are showing anger or not. The evidence of how you are behaving would lead you to update your first impression of how you were feeling.

Sometimes we human beings are not very self-aware - if our attention is focused elsewhere, we may not know how we are feeling. Also, most of the time, we aren't aware of the real reasons why we do things.

The psychologist Jonathan Haidt, in his illuminating book *The Happiness Hypothesis*, likens the mind to an elephant with a rider. The rider - our conscious self - thinks he is in control, and that he is telling the elephant what to do. Actually the elephant - which is, essentially, our unconscious mind, makes most of the decisions. If you've ever wanted with all your willpower to stop smoking, but still found yourself lighting up, you will know what I mean.

Because we want to feel like we are consistent, the rider will make up reasons after the event to explain what the elephant has done. These are usually unrelated to the real reasons. The rider isn't lying - he really believes in those made up reasons. They just usually aren't the real ones.

So if you have a problem with someone acting a certain way, asking them "Why?" will probably not get you much useful information. Even assuming they aren't trying to excuse or justify their behaviour, and they actually want to give you an honest answer, what they will give you is the rider's explanation - which probably won't be the real one.

So the only reliable information about a person is their behaviour. If you were to rely just on your intuitions about their thoughts and feelings, you might be right most of the time, but occasionally you would be mistaken because of the deletion, distortion and generalisation imposed by your mental filters. You need to update your opinions with what you observe of their behaviour.

If you were to rely on what they tell you about their thoughts, feelings and intentions, you would be getting the rider's story, which might bear no relation to their real motivations.

Consequently, it's behaviour that actually counts. The same applies to you - the only reliable information about you is what you actually do.

## Practical ways to make this principle work for you

### 1. Don't ask 'Why?'
If you're aiming to get someone to change their behaviour, don't ask 'Why?' - it won't get you useful information and may end up entrenching the behaviour.

### 2. Don't "Mind-read"
Check your guesses about other people's thoughts, feelings and motivations against their actual behaviour. Don't "mind-read" (acting as if you have certain knowledge of someone else's interior world).

### 3. Labelling a problem may conceal vital information
If you're a therapist, counsellor, coach, or consultant, don't assume that a diagnosis or label of your client's problem is all that's going on.

The 'presenting problem' - what is apparent to the client or to you at first sight - may be just a symptom of the underlying problem. Equally, it may be just one small aspect of the presenting problem that needs to change. Find out what the client is actually doing - their 'strategy for having the problem' as we term it in NLP - and let that suggest appropriate changes.

### 4. What's your standard method for deciding whether to trust someone?
Neither giving your full trust automatically, nor automatically denying trust, is a good idea. Give people opportunities to be trustworthy in small steps so you can gradually build up deserved trust.

### 5. Apply this principle to yourself
What happens when you apply the idea that behaviour is the only reliable information to yourself? Is your behaviour always consistent with your self-image, and what you say and believe your values to be? Take a moment to look actively for counter-examples, times when you did not act as you like to think you would. What have you

learned from these occasions, and how will you behave differently in similar ways in the future?

# 6

## Mind and body are one system

Let's consider another fundamental presupposition of NLP - that Mind and Body are one system. Your body, of course, is on one level a physical object. It has a position in space, it's a certain height, it has a certain weight under Earth's gravitational conditions, and so on. Your mind, on the other hand, is not in a particular physical location, has no dimensions or weight, and seems non-physical in every meaningful way.

Philosophers down the ages have wrestled with the question of how this immaterial mind or spirit controls the physical body - or is it the other way round? This question is known as the 'mind-body' problem, and I don't think they are going to resolve it any time soon.

In NLP we can look at Mind and Body in another way, one that makes that problem irrelevant. Mind and body are one system. There are flows of information exchanged between body and brain at various different levels - it's all information flows. At one level we experience these as thoughts and feelings; at a more physical level, the information is carried by electrical impulses along neurons, by neurotransmitters migrating across synaptic gaps, and by protein-like molecules called neuropeptides that communicate information and regulate various systems in the body.

There's a constant, multilevel, multi-way conversation going on between body and mind. Now since we have brain-type cells (neurons) in other places than just the brain - in the heart and the gut, for example - there's no hard and fast boundary between the mind and the body.

Most traditional systems of medicine, such as Ayurveda in India and Traditional Chinese Medicine, recognised this mind-body link. Until the middle of the last century, Western medicine didn't - until researchers started to discover certain links. So, for example, in the 1960s Herbert Benson, a professor at Harvard Medical School, discovered that meditation and the relaxation response could reduce blood pressure. Later studies have shown that stress and emotions can affect the immune system, resistance to infectious diseases, and wound healing.

If you want to learn more about this, by the way, the book *Molecules of Emotion* by Candace Pert, a neuroscience researcher who discovered the opiate receptor in brain cells.

It's not a one-way link from mind to body. For example, studies in the last few years have shown that contrary to the stereotype of the 'dumb jock', aerobic exercise improves mental focus - and even grows new brain cells in the area of the brain that controls learning and memory, something that was thought to be impossible up to the mid-90s. The great thing about the discovery of more and more pieces in the mind-body puzzle is that it identifies more and more ways in which you can make a difference to your health, your emotional well being, and the results you get. We are nowhere near being able to completely use our minds to keep our bodies in perfect health - and vice versa - contrary to what some self-help gurus might claim, but we are beginning, bit by bit, to move in that direction.

What it comes down to is this: how your body is - its state of health, how you stand, how you breathe, the way you move, what you eat - affects your mind and emotions, and vice versa. For example, it's impossible for your mind to be calm if the muscles of your body are constantly tensed, and it's very hard to be stressed if your body is fully relaxed.

It's easy to experience the mind-body link in practice. Try this quick experiment:

1. Slump over and look at your feet. Now, try to remember a time when you were happy, excited and full of energy....
2. Now, stand up, look up, and throw your arms wide - and try to remember a time that was quite boring, grey and miserable....

Notice what happened. I'm guessing that it was not easy to remember a happy time when you were slumped over, and also not easy to bring to mind a dull, miserable time when you were standing up and looking up in a posture that usually means 'exultation'.

Our minds and emotions are embodied - or to put it another way, mind and body are one system. If we didn't have human-shaped bodies, our language and the concepts we use to think with would be very different.

# Practical ways to make this principle work for you

### 1. Are you taking enough breaks at work?

Most people find that they work better and feel less stressed if they take regular breaks during the working day. However, the stressed individual may feel uncomfortable and guilty about taking breaks, even when they admit that their usual driven work patterns are causing them stress ("but the work just won't get done"). Research is beginning to establish a scientific basis for common-sense advice.

Our bodies have a Basic Rest and Activity Cycle, consisting of 90-120 minutes of activity followed by 20 minutes of rest. This cycle can easily be stretched or distorted, as when the individual works through the morning without taking a break, skips lunch, or works late. However, it has been found that people whose rest-activity cycle remains irregular for extended periods develop stress-related symptoms.

The rest-activity cycle involves alternate shifts in dominance from one side of the brain to another. When we move from activity to rest, the left side of the brain (associated with logic, sequence, details, analysis, calculation and language - "work mode") gives up dominance to the right side (associated with patterns, intuition, and emotion - "relaxation mode").

While we can force ourselves to remain in work mode for long periods, the right side of the brain eventually reasserts itself, leading to a loss of concentration and increased tiredness and error rates.

It's no accident that workplaces and schools traditionally built mid-morning and mid-afternoon breaks into their schedule; employers and school authorities found that people work better and think more clearly with regular breaks.

Sometimes a client will say to me "This won't work. I'll just have to add the time on to the end of the day so I'm working even longer hours!" Actually, no you won't. Just because you're at your desk, it doesn't mean you're doing productive work at a constant rate. If you're anything like me, you get far more done when you're feeling good, and far less done (with more mistakes) when you're tired.

By taking breaks in the middle of the morning and the middle of the afternoon, getting out of the workplace altogether at lunchtime, and leaving work at a reasonable time in the evening, you can improve the quality of your work and get more done in less time. So even if you aren't prepared to do it for the sake of your own health and sanity, you can take breaks with a clear conscience - because your employer (or clients, or customers) will benefit as well!

What happens if you don't take account of the needs of your mind-body system? Typically, if the 'arousal response' to stressful situations is prolonged over weeks or months ('chronic stress'), excess amounts of stress hormones are produced and flood the system. It seems that the cells of the body begin to shut down and destroy their receptor sites for these hormones. When the receptors are below their normal levels the person will experience withdrawal - they miss the adrenalin high and the levels of arousal and performance that go with it. They will be tempted to over-work, or use stimulants (sugar, caffeine, nicotine or other drugs) to try to regain the high.

Overachievers can become locked into a vicious circle of ever-increasing levels of activity and stress hormones - until the mind-body system 'crashes' and develops physical symptoms. You can avoid this, and sustain health and high performance indefinitely, by being aware the needs of your mind-body system to take regular breaks.

For further reference, read *The Way We're Working Isn't Working: The Four Forgotten Needs That Energize Great Performance* by Tony Schwartz.

## 2. Exercise

Various studies show that exercise lifts your mood. Where can you build more exercise into your life? You don't have to start training for a marathon if that doesn't suit you - even walking a bit more than usual is massively better than nothing.

## 3. View symptoms as messages

Notice any recurring patterns of health issues in your life. Viewing symptoms as annoyances to be ignored, or in more severe cases to be suppressed, is the traditional Western way of coping with disturbances or transitions in the mind-body system. People are encouraged to just get on with it - which up to a point is great from the point of view of getting things done, and works to the extent that many symptoms do just go away by themselves. Where symptoms persist, though, we are encouraged to suppress them.

When I lived in London there were advertisements in the London subway system along the lines of "Hard day's work? Headache? Take painkillers and enjoy your evening!" In other words, headaches and similar symptoms were presented as something to be expected as normal after every working day.

*It's as if you're the king of a vast empire, and in a far-flung border province there's a famine or a flood that's causing hardship. The people try to deal with it on their own, but eventually they send a messenger to the king to plead for help. And the king... shoots the messenger.*

*Times are still hard in the faraway province, so eventually they send a tougher, harder to kill messenger who can give the king's guard a bit more trouble. He breaks into the throne room, but the guards cut him down before he can deliver the message.*

*This goes on for some time, with ever tougher messengers being sent in ever greater numbers, and the king just refusing to listen and shooting the messengers at increasing cost. Eventually, the province is so desperate that they raise an army and revolt. And they march on the capital and besiege the palace, sending out agitators to get the rest of the empire to join the revolt.*

*And what happens next? Well, it's a little late by that point, and the king is probably wishing he'd listened to the very first messenger, but if he's smart he will finally agree to listen to the message, and make whatever changes need to be made to put things right for the stricken province.*

So, what if you looked at physical symptoms as messages from your body, trying to tell you something, rather than as annoyances to be got rid of? If the symptoms were a message, trying to tell you something, what are they trying to tell you?

"Fake it till you make it" - various bits of research suggest that deliberately adopting certain postures or facial expressions will tend to make you feel the way that is usually associated with this body language. For example, deliberately smiling really does make you feel better - especially if you also raise your cheeks to produce the crinkling round the eyes characteristic of a genuine or 'Duchenne' smile.

Also, walking like a confident person will make you feel more confident - worth remembering if you are on your way to an interview.

Contrary to what some 'motivational gurus' tell you, you don't have to feel massively motivated before you take action. Motivation tends to follow action, so the important thing is just to get started. If the thought of doing something seems overwhelming, break the task down into smaller steps, until taking the first step is a no-brainer. You'll find that you will feel more motivated to take the next step.

Finally, practising yoga, dance, or martial arts such as tai chi or aikido will help to strengthen the mind-body link, and really any form of exercise is better than nothing.

# PRINCIPLES ABOUT COMMUNICATION AND CHANGE

*"Out beyond ideas of wrongdoing and rightdoing, there is a field. I will meet you there."*
**- Jalal al-Din Muhammad Rumi, Sufi poet and philosopher (1207 - 1273)**

*"Believe there are no limits but the sky"*
**– Miguel de Cervantes (1547 - 1616)**

Next we'll consider six NLP presuppositions about communication and making changes. These will come in useful with any kind of communication, or coaching, or managing, whether it's an individual or a group that you're working with.

# 7

## Respect for the other person's model of the world

This follows directly from the idea that everyone has his or her own model of the world. If you want to communicate with someone, and especially if you want them to do something or change their minds about something, you have to start from where they are.

### A quick and easy way to demotivate your employees

When I was a fairly junior employee in a big software consultancy, we used to have a big company get-together every year. It was a welcome opportunity to catch up with workmates, as often we would be working away at far-flung client sites for months. Before the good part (a slap-up meal with free bar), we'd gather in a big hotel conference room to hear about the group's successes, watch a presentation or two on some innovative project the company was involved in, and finally the big boss would get up and give us a pep talk about how great we were and how we needed to stay smart and keep working hard.

I don't remember much about these speeches - it was over 20 years ago - but one has stuck in my mind ever since as an example of what not to do. The climax of the boss's speech - with lots of flashy PowerPoint transitions of course: "So we need to innovate and stay ahead" he said "because that's how we'll increase shareholder value."

The applause was somewhat muted. *Shareholder value?* That was *it?* That was supposed to be our motivation for working long hours and spending months away from home? Personally, I didn't care about shareholder value. I was an employee, not a shareholder. At that moment, it felt like I was working for no reason at all, and I was demotivated if anything. Why? Because the boss had not put himself in the shoes of his audience.

## Start from where the other person is standing

If you are talking to engineers, think like an engineer. If you're trying to get the finance department to let you buy a new laptop, don't go on about how technically advanced it is - show them that it will improve your productivity and save them money. If you are coaching someone, don't demand that they ditch everything they believe before they can start improving their performance.

Most of all, if you are aiming to persuade someone to change their minds, you have to start from where they are. Don't expect them to jump out of their map and join you in yours. Why would they? What's in it for them?

You have to start with seeing the world from the other person's point of view. In particular, appeal to their values. What you think is important doesn't matter to them. If they don't see your message as relevant to what they feel is important, why would they even bother listening?

## 'Resistance' is usually a lack of rapport

When people feel their map of the world is under attack, they dig in, harden their attitudes, and resist. This is particularly true if, unlike you, they are not aware of the distinction between map and territory. Of course they are going to shut you out and not listen - to them, you're talking nonsense and threatening the very existence of their viewpoint. At this point, their primary objective becomes not to change their mind.

What follows from this is that when a leader, or a coach or therapist, or a sales person meets 'resistance', that's most likely a lack of rapport. This isn't about fancy tricks to get the person into rapport with you, it's about removing the obstacles to communication. When you are in rapport with a colleague, or a client, or a customer, you take things at the pace that works for them, using language that appeals and makes sense to them, and you work from their map, so they never have to think "Hang on, that isn't right!"

If you encounter resistance through lack of rapport, the first thing you should do is pay more attention.

## The need to be "right"

I want to talk briefly about "winning" arguments and the need to be "right". When you see someone attempting to "win" an argument by grandstanding, or scoring points off their "opponent", the real message they are giving out is "I am a poor communicator". Even if they "win" the argument - in other words, they've worn the other person down so they shut up - what they are doing in the long term is storing up resentment and hardening the other person's attitudes.

Only when you start from other person's map do you give them a chance to start finding their way from where they are to where you would like them to be.

This doesn't mean giving up your map and adopting theirs as true - it just means respecting their map and working with it.

## Practical ways to make this principle work for you
If you intend to get someone to change their mind about something, try this thought experiment:

### 1. Put yourself in the shoes of your intended audience
'Become' the other person, in a 'method acting' kind of way, as much as you can. Now, staying in the character of your intended audience, ask yourself these questions:

### What's most important to me about this topic?
(People trained in NLP will recognise this as a question to elicit a person's values)

### Why is that important to me?
This will give you an idea of their motivation. Are they motivated *towards* benefits and possibilities, or *away from* problems and things that could go wrong?

### What do I already believe about this topic?
(actually your audience probably thinks in terms of "What do I know to be true about this topic?")

### 2. Now come back to yourself
Bring back everything that you've learned from that exercise (while remembering that it's only guesswork - you still need to check your intuitions against your audience's actual behaviour, since behaviour is the only reliable evidence about a person).

In the light of that tentative information, ask yourself these questions:

What knowledge is assumed in order to make sense of your argument?

Does your audience actually have this knowledge?

If not, how will you get that information across to them in a credible way?

## 3. Does your message fit with your audience's belief systems?

What values and beliefs does your argument appeal to?

What emotions are you aiming to evoke?

Are these values and beliefs shared by your audience?

How are you going to preframe your argument to appeal to their existing values?

## 4. Establishing credibility

Is there anything in your argument that seems wrong or will not make sense to your audience? If so, change it.

Are you using any jargon that will alienate your audience or seem like you're talking down to them? If so, change it.

And - this is particularly true in business situations like pitches and presentations - from their point of view, how credible are you as a speaker on this topic? How will you establish your credibility?

## 5. Getting beyond persuasion

Finally, and this goes beyond persuasion or advocacy and into openness and learning, what can you take from their map of the world to enrich yours? What can you learn from the conversation?

# 8

## The "meaning" of communication is the response you get

Have you ever paid someone a compliment, and they've taken it as a put-down? Have you ever said something intended to make someone laugh, and they've taken it as a hurtful comment? Have you ever tried to make that kind of situation better, and just found that you're just digging yourself deeper?

### How to destroy your business in two minutes

Let's take a riches-to-rags example. In 1991 Gerald Ratner was a successful UK businessman who had transformed his family's jewellery business from a rather stuffy, old-fashioned retailer to a very successful chain with a branch on nearly every high street. He shocked the jewellery industry by putting up fluorescent orange posters advertising cut-price bargains and "3 for 2" offers. The shops were kind of tacky but the public loved it, and the chain expanded rapidly.

Then everything changed. As a high-profile retail wizard, he was invited to give a speech at the Institute of Directors. He had a standard speech that he'd used for five years or so, with some jokes that always went down well, like this one:

*We also do cut-glass sherry decanters complete with six glasses on a silver-plated tray that your butler can serve you drinks on, all for £4.95. People say, "How can you sell this for such a low price?" I say, "Because it's total crap."*

and...

*We even sell a pair of gold earrings for under £1, which is cheaper than a prawn sandwich from Marks & Spencer. But I have to say that the sandwich will probably last longer than the earrings.*

(Reported in the Daily Telegraph - see www.bit.ly/ratner-speech)

As usual, the speech went down fine with his immediate audience of fellow businessmen. But the next day, the tabloid press were accusing him of insulting his customers. "YOU 22 CARAT GOLD MUGS" was the Daily Mirror's headline.

What was intended as a bit of self-deprecating fun, and was taken that way by his intended audience of high-powered business owners, was taken in quite another way by his customers - at that time struggling with job losses, house repossessions, and just making ends meet in the recession of the early 90s. They took it personally. To them, here was this fat cat worth £350 million, with a yacht, a private plane, and lots of houses, mocking the people who had put him there. Gerald's protestations that it was a private function that he didn't expect to be reported, and that the remarks were not intended to be taken seriously, made him look even more out of touch.

The response of his customers was about what you would expect from someone who had been mocked. They stopped buying Ratners jewellery. The value of the company plummeted by around £500 million and it very nearly collapsed. He resigned the following year, and the company changed its name to the Signet Group.

## How to avoid being misunderstood

What was going on there? Well, we know about mental filters, deletion, distortion, and generalisation. When you say something, or write an email, to another person, your words are being interpreted through their mental filters. They are also judging your non-verbal communication - the tone of your voice, your facial expression, and body language - through those same filters. Of course, with emails, you don't have body language or voice tone, so the reader has to fill in that missing information as best they can from their own map of the world - which is why people can frequently take emails the wrong way.

By the time the other person is aware of your communication, it's already been through their filters. So to them, their interpretation of your message *is* the message itself.

Sometimes, if your maps of the world are fairly similar, the message they receive is pretty close to the message you thought you were sending. The information from their map that they use to fill in the deletions the message is pretty much the same as the information that you were leaving out, and so on.

If you're working from diverging maps, the message they receive can be very different from the one you thought you were sending. And since you are communicating with them with some sort of desired response in mind, it's the message as they receive it that's important.

Since you don't know for sure what their filters are, the only way you can know if your message has been received as sent is to notice what their response is. If their response is not what you expected from the message you sent, that means it's been received differently, and you've communicated something other than what you intended.

### Don't act like "the Englishman abroad"
Imagine the classic stereotype of the Englishman abroad, trying to ask directions from a passer by who doesn't speak English. The time-honoured tactic of repeating the same question, but louder, while thinking "Why can't this person speak English?" is not going to work. Learning a few words of the local language, or trying a bit of sign language, will probably get you a lot further.

As the communicator, it's your responsibility to change how you are sending the message - whether that's a change in wording, voice tone, body language, or the medium you send it by, until you get the response that tells you your message has been received as sent.

As a listener or a recipient of communication, you will be more likely to jump to conclusions when you remember that what you are hearing or reading is your filtered interpretation of the message. This is particularly worth remembering with email communications, where the body language and voice tone that normally supply the emotional context to make sense of the message are not available, and you've only got the words to go on.

## Practical ways to make this principle work for you

### 1. First of all, know what response you are looking for
What's the purpose of your communication? Are you looking to get the other person to change their behaviour, to change how they feel, to reassure them, to impart some information, or just to establish, maintain or strengthen a connection with them? You won't know if your communication has been 'received as sent' if you are unclear about what you wanted to communicate.

### 2. Notice the non-verbal signals
Pay attention to the non-verbal signals or 'paralanguage' that you get from the other person. The non-verbal response always comes before

the verbal one, but you won't notice it unless you pay attention. In a conversation, your attention should mostly be on the other person, rather than, for example, in your own head, trying to predict what they might say next or worrying about how you are coming across.

## 3. If your communication isn't working, vary it

If what you saying is not getting the response you want, say it another way - and keep getting your message across in different ways until it gets the response you want.

## 4. Treat unexpected responses as feedback

If you've taken into account the principle of 'Respect for the other person's model of the world' that we discussed earlier, you should already be getting better responses to your communication. If you get an unexpected or unwanted response, that's useful feedback telling you to check your understanding of their model of the world against their response, and update your understanding if necessary.

Is what you have said in line with their values? Does your message make sense in their map of the world? Did you express yourself in language that they can understand, and that is congruent with who you are? People are very good at spotting incongruence - think of the jarring note that you get when a middle aged person in a position of authority uses, or misuses, teenage slang in an attempt to seem down with the kids.

Or - and this happens from time to time even with the best communicators, although it happens much less when you are sincere and congruent about what you are saying - did you just make a slip, and need to apologise for it or to correct the false impression?

# 9

## You cannot not communicate

We are constantly communicating, in everything we do. Even staying silent is a communication, especially where the other person is expecting to say something.

**7% - 38% - 55%: the facts**
You don't just communicate in words. You may have heard the statistic that only 7% of the meaning of what you say is the words you use, 38% is conveyed by voice tone, and 55% by body language. What most people don't know is that these statistics have been taken wildly out of context and are often misused.

Originally these figures come from research into nonverbal communication done by the psychologist Albert Mehrabian. He asked people to judge how a speaker was feeling by listening to a recording of a single word spoken in different tones of voice. He used positive words: ""dear", "thanks" and "honey", neutral words: "maybe", "oh", and "really", and 'negative' words: "brute", "don't", "terrible". And he had his speakers read the words in positive, neutral and 'negative' tones of voice. He found that where the word and the voice tone were inconsistent, more listeners went with the voice tone than the meaning of the word when judging how the speaker was feeling.

In a second experiment, his speakers read out one neutral word ("maybe") in the three different tones, and at the same time the listeners were shown photos of positive, neutral or negative facial expressions.

Putting the results of the two experiments together, he concluded that words, voice tone, and facial expression (not body language as a whole) were important in the proportion 7%, 38% and 55% - but this figure is only applicable to how the listener judges the feelings of the speaker, only when the speaker only uses one word, and only when the voice tone is inconsistent with the meaning of the word or voice tone is inconsistent with facial expression. That's not a combination of circumstances that happens very often in the real world, so it's a bit of a leap to apply it to the whole meaning of a communication. It's also worth noting that neither of the experiments studied all three communication channels together.

So that statistic has been taken wildly out of context, and it is meaningless when applied to communication as a whole, but you still hear it a lot. A friend of mine was at a course where the trainer trotted out that "93% of communication is non-verbal" myth, and - knowing that it doesn't help the other students to make the trainer look stupid, even when they say something that's wrong - she waited until the break and mentioned privately to him that the research doesn't actually support the statistic. He suggested that she didn't know what she was talking about, and that her 4-year psychology degree was worthless. She left it at that.

But in the afternoon, the trainer seems to have decided to make himself look big by making her look small. He held her up in front of the class as an example of a Luddite, someone who "refuses to believe the latest research that proves communication is 93% non-verbal." Big mistake... she challenged him to do the rest of the day's training using only body language and voice tone - since he'd still be communicating 93% of the information. So he ended up communicating a message about himself that he hadn't meant to.

## How non-verbal communication modifies what you say

And yet, the reason that you still hear those figures so often is that on the face of it they sort of sound as if they should be right, even if they don't stand up when you think about them. Voice tone and facial expression or body language can modify the meaning of what you say. Think of the difference between what a sincere compliment sounds like, and the same words delivered in a sarcastic tone.

Nonverbal communication - 'paralinguistics' as psychologists call it - forms the context against which the listener evaluates the meaning of the words, and how sincere you are. While the words convey a message about whatever it is you're talking about, the non-verbal communication around it is conveying messages about your relationship with the listener, and how you feel about what you're saying.

All the time, then, our facial expressions, body language, posture, and voice tone are sending messages which people around us are interpreting, whether they are conscious of it or not. They use those interpretations to form guesses about how you're feeling, what you are thinking, your intentions, and what you are likely to do next.

People can sometimes send very obvious messages by doing or saying nothing. Sometimes this is appropriate, sometimes not. If your team are looking to you for leadership in a time of crisis, and you stay in your office with the door closed, that's sending a message. If someone makes a racist or sexist joke, and they are expecting you to laugh or at least smile, not doing that is sending another message. And if someone is trying to provoke you, and you don't rise to it, that's also sending a message.

The key is to be aware that whatever you do or don't do, you're always communicating, and the meaning of that communication depends as much on the context as on what you are saying or not saying.

## Practical ways to make this principle work for you

### 1. Be clear about what you want to communicate
Put yourself in the shoes of your intended audience, and look at what you are intending to do and the manner in which you are intending to do it, from their point of view. What, from their point of view, are you actually communicating?

### 2. The messages you send are not just the words you use
The clothes you wear, the way you stand, the tone of your voice, all convey a message to your audience that modifies the meanings they take from your words. So ask yourself: is my non-verbal communication appropriate to my audience? Is it congruent with the verbal message I want to put across.

### 3. Sometimes not responding at all is a useful communication
The idea of behavioural reinforcement, which came originally from animal training, suggests that any response you give to a particular behaviour, even an angry or discouraging one, may serve to reinforce that behaviour, so the other person, or the dog or whatever, is more likely to do it again. Why? Because at least they got a response from you.

You see this with other people's parenting skills sometimes (never your own, of course) - a small child that's ignored will eventually do something to provoke the parent into yelling at or slapping them, because any response is better than being ignored. And the more wound up the parent gets, the more the child acts up. The parent's response is unintentionally reinforcing the behaviour.

So think about what behaviour you want to reinforce, and what you want to ignore. This would apply to your children, your partner, your employees, your pets, or even your boss. Make sure that you reinforce behaviour that you want - don't just ignore it. And if your normal irritable response to certain behaviours isn't working, try ignoring it and see what happens.

# 10

## There is no failure, only feedback

"What does this mean?" you might be thinking. "Of course there's such a thing as failure!"

Well, of course there is - if you choose to look at it that way. If you do, please remember that the concept of failure is not a real, physical thing in the real world - it's what academics call a 'construct', something that's made up by the human mind. It's a particular way of labelling certain events, one of many possible ways.

Since it's our minds that have come up with the concept of failure, I think we have the right to ask how well this concept serves us. It turns out that it isn't that helpful. In the context of evaluating your own actions, or those of people who report to you, it's actually harmful.

Let's say you try out some new action or new way of doing things, and it doesn't work as you had hoped. If you think, "that failed", you might also think that you failed. From there, it's only a short step to thinking of yourself as a failure. And once you think of yourself in those terms, what are you going to expect to happen the next time you try something new?

**Why it pays to think experimentally**
It's much more useful to think of taking a new action in terms of an experiment. You try something out. It either works as you want it to, in which case great, you can keep doing it; or, it doesn't work as you want it to, in which case you have gained valuable feedback from your environment - the universe, as my "new age" friends call it - which is telling you to do something different.

That's all that this presupposition means. You can choose how you look at the results you get. People who frame unexpected or unwanted results as failure tend to get discouraged, lose interest, and give up, and may be so demoralised that they don't learn from the experience; when you view such results as useful feedback, you learn from what happens, modify what you are doing, keep doing that until you get the result you want - or an even better one.

### "Fixed" mindset or "Growth" mindset?

It's nice to see this idea getting some backup from academic research. The Stanford psychologist Carol Dweck has been researching mindset, performance and motivation for 40 years. Her key finding is that if you believe your intelligence and talent are fixed (what she calls a "fixed" mindset), your main motivation will be to look good and you will avoid challenges and feedback that might tarnish your image; whereas if you believe you can develop your ability (a "growth" mindset), you will value learning, relish challenges, welcome feedback and keep going through setbacks.

The fixed mindset thinks in black and white terms of success or failure. If a person's confidence is based on their ability, and they believe that ability is fixed, then when they hit a setback - as inevitably happens from time to time - it's going to pull the rug out from under them, and they might think: "I must not be so smart after all, if I failed at this". When that happens, a person flips from believing "I can" to "I can't" very easily.

This doesn't happen with a growth mindset. When you have a growth mindset, you treat setbacks as a cue to put more effort in. Dweck and her collaborator Carol Diener found that some children with a growth mindset didn't label their failures as setbacks at all - as Diener says in an article in the Stanford Magazine (online at tiny.cc/growth-mindset):

*Failure is information—we label it failure, but it's more like, "This didn't work, I'm a problem solver, and I'll try something else."*

In other words: there is no failure, only feedback.

## Practical ways to make this principle work for you

### 1. Re-evaluate past "failures"

Look back at anything in your life that you've labelled as a "failure". What happens if instead, you label it as "useful feedback"? If you have been in the habit of thinking in terms of failure, it's worth investing some time in this exercise - it will be time well spent.

## 2. Ask "What do I need to learn?"

One great way to take on board the feedback that the world is giving you is this: any time things don't turn out how you want, ask yourself "What do I need to learn from this?" and leave some time and space for the answer to come to you. This is worth doing even, or perhaps especially, when what has happened seems to be a complete accident, since we are never fully aware of how our actions affect others around us and lead to unintended consequences. Do people who do stupid things realise they are acting stupidly? Often they don't - but if they ask themselves this question when the results come in, at least they would give themselves a chance of learning from experience.

## 3. Beware the wrong kind of praise

Carol Dweck's research into 'fixed' and 'growth' mindsets found that it's not just criticism that holds people back and installs limiting beliefs. The wrong kind of praise can also children whose parents praised them for qualities, like being intelligent or pretty, tended to grow up with fixed mindsets. By contrast, if they were praised for the effort they put in, they had more of a growth mindset. So if you want to encourage a growth mindset in your kids or your employees, praise and encourage them for their effort and attitude, rather than for qualities. And make sure you do the same for yourself in your own internal dialogue or self-talk.

# 11

## The more complex the situation you have to cope with, the more behavioural flexibility you need ("The Law of Requisite Variety")

This presupposition is derived from systems theory - the study of self-regulating systems. William Ross Ashby originally formulated the law to apply to controllers trying to keep a system stable - like the thermostat in a central heating system, to choose a very simple example. To put it into non-technical language, the law can be stated as: "the more options the controller has, the better able it is to deal with fluctuations in the system".

Regrettably, in personal development circles we sometimes see this principle reduced to the idea that "the person with the greatest flexibility wins" - so the most flexible salesperson will be the one who closes the sale, or the most flexible manager will get their own way most often. This is a massive over-simplification. In his book *Whispering In The Wind* (for hardcore NLP enthusiasts only), John Grinder points out that as any therapist knows, the idea of 'controlling' interaction with another human being is extremely optimistic.

### What doomed the dinosaurs
Really, the principle is more about adaptability and dealing with change. Think about dinosaurs. There were all kinds of shapes and sizes to make the most of various environmental niches. You had huge ones like the brontosaurus with long necks to browse from the tops of trees, you had horned ones like triceratops for browsing on grassland and seeing off predators, you had armoured spiky ones like ankylosaurus which were like living tanks.

During the last days when dinosaurs ruled the earth, the ancestors of mammals - our ancestors - were little furry animals resembling mice or shrews. They weren't particularly specialised - they couldn't run fast, they weren't big enough to be good at fighting, they didn't have wings or horns or armour. They pretty much kept out of the dinosaurs' way.

Then, for whatever reason, the climate changed. Food became scarcer - and of course it takes a lot of food to keep something as big as a dinosaur going. As they became scarcer, their predators, like the huge Tyrannosaurus Rex, also died out - there just wasn't enough food available to sustain predators of that size.

The mammals survived because they were adaptable. They could eat pretty much anything, their coats and warm blood kept them warm, they had short reproductive cycles so they could recover quickly from population impacts when conditions improved again. They survived, and took over, because they had more options open to them.

So the "Law of Requisite Variety" in NLP is more about being able to adapt to change than about having to win everything. We might summarise it as "The more complex the situation you have to cope with, the more behavioural flexibility you need", or even "If what you are doing isn't working, do something different".

## Practical ways to make this principle work for you

### 1. If you're stuck, change your frame

In any situation where you feel that you have run out of options, start thinking laterally. What do other people do in similar situations? What would you do if you didn't care what people thought, or even - and I'm not a big fan of this saying as a general principle (just look what it did to Enron) but it may be useful in this case - "what would you do if you knew you couldn't fail?"

### 2. Look at what's on the far side of the block

If you're limiting your options by thinking "I couldn't do that", ask yourself "What would happen if I did?"

Sometimes we scare ourselves with vague thoughts of terrible consequences which turn out to be not so terrible when we examine them - just like the unseen monster in a horror film which isn't so scary once you see it.

## 3. Vary your routine

Habits can become a powerful restriction if left unchallenged. Develop your flexibility by doing something different occasionally. Take a different route into work, brush your teeth using your non-dominant hand, if you're a conservative read a lefty newspaper occasionally, and vice versa. Your life will be more interesting as well.

## 4. Get comfortable with confusion

Notice how well you tolerate ambiguity - in other words, how comfortable are you when you don't know exactly what's going on? Developmental psychologists tell us that people tend to become more tolerant of ambiguity, less rigid in their thinking, as they mature - although they can start becoming more rigid again in old age if they don't watch out.

People who are not comfortable with ambiguity tend to interpret it as a threat - which means they go into a less resourceful state any time they are confronted with new information that might require them to update their worldview. The temptation for them is to jump to conclusions prematurely, and as Tad James says, premature closure is as bad as premature... well never mind.

So if you're learning something new, and you feel confused, remind yourself that it's OK - confusion is just what you feel when you're taking on new information that you haven't fully made sense of yet. Confusion is a prelude to understanding. Feeling anxious or threatened by confusion is just going to put the person into a bad state that makes it harder for them to learn - so any time you feel confused, just breathe and relax.

# 12

## Any changes should increase choice and wholeness, and be evaluated in terms of ecology

Following on from the "Law of Requisite Variety", we can say that choice is better than no choice. The more options we have in our behavioural repertoire, the more likely we are to be able to make the right choice for any given situation. Also, when conditions change, it's good to have the flexibility that additional options give us.

For example, a lot of independent trainers and consultants I know have seen a drop in their business in the last couple of years, where the old ways they used to get clients have stopped working. One way they could do something about that would be to pick up the phone and start calling prospects. But they won't do it, because that behaviour is just not part of their repertoire and they don't feel it would be "them" - even though in some circumstances it may be the very best way to increase or even save their business. If only they had that additional choice available to them - if they could do something different to what isn't working any more - they could start reaching more people and making their lives better.

So any changes we make should increase choice. Remember the presupposition that "All behaviour is the best choice currently available"? By now you may be starting to see how these presuppositions fit together. You may remember that we used the example of smoking as a behaviour that a person's conscious mind might want to stop, but nevertheless they don't always find it easy to quit, because at the unconscious level they may be getting some payoff or benefit from it - "secondary gain" as it's called in therapy.

### How not to help someone quit smoking

When I ran a hypnotherapy practice, one of the clients told me about her brother, who had been to see an old-school hypnotherapist who specialised in smoking cessation and worked mostly through authoritarian hypnosis and - let's be frank - fear. He got the brother into trance, ran through his smoking cessation script, and near the end implanted this suggestion:

**"And if you ever pick up a cigarette again, you will find that you are smoking five times as much as you used to."**

What could possibly go wrong? I think you may guess what happened next. The brother stopped smoking, but a few months later he was at a party, had a few drinks, and out of habit accepted a cigarette that someone offered him. Before he knew it, he was indeed back on the cigarettes again, smoking five times as many as he used to. Not an ideal solution.

The NLP approach to change accepts that any behaviour could be useful in some context, although the situations in which smoking would be the best choice are pretty rare. With this in mind, we aim to add better choices rather than take away or prohibit the problematic choice. So with smoking, part of what you might do is to establish what, if any, is the secondary gain from smoking, and help the person to generate better choices that they can use instead of smoking in those situations where previously they used to smoke.

If you have better options that give you the same or better payoffs as the old problem behaviour, but without the downside, of course you will always choose the better options - even though the previous behaviour is still available to you. Plus, you still have the previous behaviour in your set of choices if circumstances change and it becomes useful again.

## Wholeness is better than fragmentation

Change should also aim to preserve or increase wholeness. This principle originated from therapy, where - following Virginia Satir and Fritz Perls - the early NLP pioneers did a lot of work with the idea of "parts" of someone's personality being responsible for problems, and talking directly to that part. They even got to the point of installing new parts. A side-effect of this can be that the more you treat the parts as real - rather than just convenient metaphors - the more of a life of their own they can take on. So before someone takes a decision, they have to sit down and listen to each part in turn, in the hope that they can all reach agreement.

I understand there are even some therapists in America - not NLP ones, I'm happy to say - who find that every single client they see has multiple personality disorder. If not when they start therapy, then by the time they leave.

In organisations, there are also costs involved with the old fashioned model where communication is mainly up and down, between managers and the people who report to them, rather than across the organisation between departments. Many organisations I've worked with in the UK, especially in the public sector, complain about "siloisation", where staff in different departments don't know each other, don't communicate with each other, and the left hand doesn't know what the right hand is doing. In the worst cases you get turf wars, withholding of knowledge, and departments competing for budgets, forgetting the big picture that they all work for the same organisation and are supposed to be working towards the same goals.

Any fragmentation increases costs and disrupts communication, so changes need to promote wholeness and heal unnecessary divisions.

### Is the change "ecological"?

Finally, change should be evaluated in terms of "ecology". This term has a slightly different meaning in NLP than it does in science and everyday life (the study of the relationships that living organisms have with each other and with their environment). In NLP, "ecology" is about looking at the wider impacts of changes on the wider systems - family, community and so on - of which you are a part. This is to make sure that the change is something you would still want when you look beyond the immediate context where its made - so if you are thinking of taking a new job, for example, you should consider not just the step up and the extra money, but also commuting time, what hours you will be working, the impact on your time with your family, how closely the new job aligns with your values, and the opportunities it will give you to learn, along with many other considerations.

## Practical ways to make this principle work for you

### 1. Notice any conflicts within yourself

Very often, inner conflict comes from holding two values that appear to contradict each other; for example, you might value both "excitement" and "security" in your career. So, should you take that job shark fishing in the Pacific, or stay working in the bank? There are patterns within NLP which broadly come under the heading of "parts integration" to help you resolve conflicts like this, but if you don't have a skilled NLP practitioner to hand, here's what you can do.

Ask yourself: what is it about your current situation that means you can't satisfy both values at the same time? Ask yourself what would have to happen to make it possible to satisfy both values at the same time. Then make it happen.

## 2. Look for the common higher value on both sides of a conflict

Take one of the clashing values and ask yourself: "If I have that value fully, what would that give me that is even more important than that?" This should give you a higher (more important and bigger-picture) value. Continue to ask the same question until you can't get any higher. Then do the same thing with the value on the other side. You may find that the two original values have higher values which are the same, or at least more compatible.

## 3. How to identify inner conflicts in others

You'll find that you can notice when other people have conflicting impulses quite easily - they might say things like "One the one hand I want to do this, on the other hand I want to do that..." or "I feel torn between..." or "I don't know whether to do this, or that" or even "I'm in two minds about it."

## 4. Put your goals through an "ecology check"

If you're setting a goal or a target for yourself, or your team, make sure you take into account the knock-on and systemic effects as well as your desired end result. Although your goal may be about a particular area of your life or business, it will also affect other areas. You need to take into account the consequences of achieving your goal on every other area of your life, on people close to you, and on the larger communities of which you are a part. Only then can you be sure that you really want the goal.

What will it cost you to achieve the goal? Sometimes there are costs to achieving a goal, in terms of time, effort, or what you will have to give up. Ask these questions to make sure your goal is worth what it will cost you:

"What will happen when you have it?"

"What won't happen when you have it?"

"Are there any downsides to achieving it?"

What are the wider effects of achieving your goal? Any significant goal will have an impact on the balance of your life - think this impact through now to avoid unforeseen consequences later.

"How would having this outcome affect each area of your life?"

"How would having this outcome affect the people you care about?"

"How would you having this outcome affect the wider communities of which you are a part?"

# REVIEW

*"By three methods we may learn wisdom. First, by reflection, which is noblest; second, by imitation, which is easiest, and third by experience, which is the bitterest."*

## - Confucius (Kong Qiu) (551 BC - 479 BC)

*"First say to yourself what you would be; and then do what you have to do."*

## - Epictetus (55 AD - 135 AD)

### A reminder of all the principles

In this book we have considered six presuppositions or principles about people:

1. The map is not the territory
2. All behaviour is the best choice currently available
3. People have all the resources they need to succeed
4. I am in charge of my mind, and therefore my results
5. The only reliable information about a person is behaviour
6. Mind and body are one system

And also six presuppositions about communication and change:

7. Respect for the other person's model of the world
8. The "meaning" of communication is the response you get
9. You cannot not communicate
10. There is no failure, only feedback
11. The more complex the situation you have to cope with, the more behavioural flexibility you need (the "Law of Requisite Variety")
12. Any changes should increase choice and wholeness, and be evaluated in terms of ecology.

Notice what differences you could make to your life if you take these principles on board and start acting as if they are true. Imagine what results you might get. And of course, when you start to act from these presuppositions, they quickly begin to generate their own evidence, so you really can start to get congruent about them.

# USING NLP PRINCIPLES TO RESOLVE PROBLEMS

*"The unexamined life is not worth living for a human being."*
**- Socrates, (470 BC - 399 BC)**

Just before you start your adventure in living according to these principles, here is an exercise that you can try yourself, to really understand how relevant they are to your life.

a)  Pick three of these NLP presuppositions. They could be ones that particularly resonate with you, or you could just pick any three at random.

b)  Now think of some challenge that you have - it could be at work or at home, it could be something that holds you back or more about how you are going to learn something or reach a particular target. And, by the way, if you don't have any challenges in your life, maybe you're not setting your sights high enough.

c)  Take the first of the presuppositions and use it as a lens to look at the issue. What's different about the issue when you look at it from the viewpoint of this presupposition? What options does it open up? What does it make sense to do in the light of the presupposition?

d)  Now repeat this exercise with the other two presuppositions. Notice what insights and learnings you get. The chances are that some of the insights you get will be more useful than others... so which insights are most useful to you? And what are you going to do differently as a result what you've learned?

# WHAT NOW?

*"One of the illusions of life is that the present hour is not the critical, decisive hour. Write it on your heart that every day is the best day of the year."*

**-Ralph Waldo Emerson (1803 - 1882)**

If you are interested in live NLP training, contact me and I can possibly recommend a reliable trainer near to you. If the demand is there I could be tempted to travel to wherever you are in the world and run a course myself!

To learn more about NLP, listen to my Practical NLP Podcast. For details of how to listen on iTunes and other platforms visit www.nlppod.com. This is also the site to visit for more tips, book reviews, research news and information about NLP and related subjects. You can also subscribe to the free Practical NLP Tips Newsletter there.

Visit my other website, www.coachingleaders.co.uk, for information about Emotional Intelligence, Appreciative Inquiry, leadership and coaching.

You can follow me on Twitter at www.twitter.com/PracticalNLP.

Finally, if you have any questions or feedback about this book, please do contact me at andy@coachingleaders.co.uk

Andy Smith
Cheissoux November 2017

# ABOUT THE AUTHOR

Andy Smith is an NLP trainer, Emotional Intelligence coach and Appreciative Inquiry consultant who trains and coaches director-level clients in the UK, the Middle East, and South East Asia. He specialises in helping leaders and teams get beyond the blocks that stop them achieving their potential.

Andy is the author of *Achieve Your Goals: Strategies To Transform Your Life* (Dorling Kindersley 2006) and the *Practical NLP, Practical Coaching Guides* and *Quick Personal Development* e-book series. To see all of Andy's books and e-books on Amazon, visit his author page at:

Author.to/AndySmith

Andy is a serial NLP practice group founder. He started the Richmond NLP Group (along with Nick Driscoll) in 1996 and it's still going strong, having been through a couple of changes of management. He also started the Manchester NLP Group and the Manchester Business NLP and Emotional Intelligence Group, all of which have given countless people their first step on their NLP journey.

As well as the Practical NLP e-book series, Andy has developed an acclaimed activity pack for NLP trainers, *The NLP Trainer's Exercise Pack*, as well as customisable and rebrandable NLP course manuals that will save newly-qualified trainers weeks of effort. You can find these resources at webstore.coachingleaders.co.uk.

ANDY SMITH

29190932R00042

Printed in Poland
by Amazon Fulfillment
Poland Sp. z o.o., Wrocław